the abstract god

the abstract god

albert klassen

the abstract god

Publisher: DEE ELL PUBLISHING

ISBN: 978-1-7782809-5-5

Further information: albertklassen@icloud.com

Books by Albert Klassen

the death of the girl with the beautiful hair
looking at life from an angle
the life of lido pepperman
the church
radical madness
a monk in paradise
the abstract god
journey
never been to berlin

Chapter One

who invented the God we call Yahweh
and told us we had to obey
and put our trust in him
instead of a guy named Kim

this God created the earth and the sky
and had a say in when we die
knowing everything he was supreme
the head of a heavenly team

the bible is our record of this great Lord
who demanded that everyone get on board
and worship him alone
bowing low before his throne

the Bible and Josephus say the earth is 6000 years
old
that's the bill of goods that we've been sold
but the scientists say that it's not true
that it took billions of years to develop this stew

they point to fossils and layers of rock
and the proof of the carbon clock
then there is evolution and all that stuff
of Christian fables they've had quite enough

the editorial staff in heaven sent the bible down in
code
to be set down by men of God in an earthly mode
then it was gathered together by the scribes
who as it happened were taking heavenly bribes

taking a little license with what they imagined they
received
adding little flourishes to embellish how it would be
perceived
hoping in the end that it all made sense
these spiritual stories that they thought was their
duty to dispense

there had been many gods before old Yahweh
but they vanished after they'd had their day
imaginations were always on fire
with many pants on fire on the telephone wire

aside from humans penchant for complaining
they always felt the need for some explaining
why this and why that
and why not to trust a big black cat

superstition is a characteristic we all share
scared and nervous we stop and stare
at mysterious happenings in the sky
and shake our heads and wonder why

master master up above
do you mankind really love
what meaneth thunder lightning and the snow
are you trying something to show

us feeble humans lie in chains
why do you take such pains
to punish us for every sin
is it because you have to win

you make us grovel underneath your heel
you seem to rejoice when you make us squeal
why would you want to torture us in hell
casting upon us such an evil spell

God has been associated with a snow white dove
and accused of being a God of love
but when you kill most humans in a flood
your face begins to look like mud

in the garden it began for all of us
that's where God invented the Volkswagen bus
Adam was the driver and Eve was his maid
one day he kissed her and got himself laid

God wasn't happy and kicked them out
Eve was pissed and began to pout
so he cursed her with periods and planted all those
weeds
it was punishment for all their evil deeds

they did horrible things like eating a forbidden fruit
good heavens it's not like they stole some loot
God was mad as hell and out of control
and cursed all of mankind and put them in a hole

he damned all of mankind cause Eve picked the fruit
Satan was laughing he thought it was a hoot
what's wrong with you he scoffed at God
you really are a cruel old sod

for mankind it wasn't a great start
it looked like God didn't have a heart
treating Adam and Eve so unkind
and leaving them all alone and so maligned

in the beginning was the word
in the beginning it was so absurd
in the beginning a punishment had occurred
in the beginning the lines got blurred

and so time went by and God liked a man called
abram
he told him not to eat any ham
cause ham was sinful and unclean and bad
even though it was the latest fad

God liked things to be good and pure
he didn't like the leper or the whore
he demanded sacrifices killed upon an altar
and then consecrated by a priest called walter

blood he said would wash away all sin
why not just drink a little gin
as you sit upon the stools
and utter prayers like some kinds of fools

mother Mary perfect and sweet
help me as I sit upon my seat
give me wisdom so that I
will never ever tell a big fat lie

how could one god the universe make
it seems this story is a fake
the whole thing seems like a fairytale to me
how could all this be

there was a snake that talked
it was a story that really rocked
but my friends what can we do
this story just ain't true

I'm not going to throw away my common sense
and buy this load of nonsense
it's just not cool
to be such a stupid fool

on paper you can draw the God you desire
and make him invent sin and hellfire
but that doesn't make him come to life
or allow him to cut you with a knife

everything can be made to fit your dream
as you sit and eat your pink ice cream
but reality has its own set of rules
and when you break them you look like fools

many gods have come and gone
with millions of followers falling for the con
in the end they've all been wrong
even though they looked so strong

Chapter Two

in the bible there was a lot of begatting
God was doing a lot of formatting
Abraham begat Isaak and Isaak begat Jacob
whose children formed the Israeli club

the Israelites were gods chosen race
it's them that the Egyptians did chase
but they drowned in the Red Sea
while the Jews escaped and were free

and so they came to the promised land
after eating a lot of manna that God supplied on
demand
the land flowed with milk and honey and apple pie
supplied by the father in the big blue sky

God said kill all the people in this place
and then dress up in gold and lace
and make a feast to celebrate your land
that you received from my almighty hand

who cares if the children are crying as you kill
who cares if the mothers are wailing as you kill
who cares if the men are screaming as you kill
it's my command and it's my will

oh ya this is a God of love
his symbol is a snow white dove
it makes me sick to read this stuff
God is an invented terrorist and I've had quite
enough

quit saying that he's merciful and kind
he's the opposite with a killer mind
unfair capricious and barbaric to boot
this god is someone who I'd like to shoot

the apologists hover around this shit like flies
trying to justify all these lies
but holy smokes they're wasting their time
trying to whitewash all this grime

they manipulate words and meanings they do twist
so no one can even get the gist
of what was said and when and how
while they go eat some Roman chow

eat and drink you apologist scums
you're all just a bunch of bums
you take a tale and make it even worse
for that I put on you a curse

you deceive the masses as you vie for power
eating pizza pie and going to the shower
and you can scrub and scrub for all you're worth
you'll always smell like dogshit and earth

that an old man with a long white beard
creates the entire universe is just weird
it says that through the garden God walked
and as he walked he talked

they didn't call God a she
no they called him a he
we don't know if god ate kale
but he was definitely male

we know that even if a single male had a special
touch
he couldn't create much
so here we see that the bible did dispense
a bunch of pure nonsense

what did they know in those days of yore
today we know a whole lot more
and we should know when we hear a fairy tale
with juicy tidbits up for sale

step right up got a great story to tell
bout a fall from grace and a place called hell
another God is stepping out
let's all stand up and scream and shout

and what religion would be complete without a great
city
on whom this God could take pity
and promise to redeem
and so fulfill the messiah dream

Jerusalem was God's city so holy and great
that so many Gentiles loved to hate
he promised to destroy it and then build it up again
it all sounds so silly and insane

how can one male God hear everyone as they pray
how can he know what they have to say
how can he be aware of all that goes on
how can he know when somethings gone

it's a miracle and we can't understand
and we don't have the right to demand
an explanation for all this activity
especially about the nativity

but so many buy it all
they don't even make a call
to check it out and show some doubt
and find out what's it's all about

oh no it's tradition and we're all in
we must go to hell because of Adam's sin
so unworthy and filthy and rotten
it's time for everyone to go and pick some cotton

swing low
ho ho
grab a chariot and fly the coop
then off to the parlour for a scoop

in the image of God did he make man
calling him Adam and not Stan
it was like God that man looked
but then he sinned and his goose was cooked

to condemn any person at the moment of birth
for that there cannot be any mirth
it's a human rights abuse
for which we have no use

how can God defend such a move
he was clearly in a sinister groove
as God he should have known what is right
he was clearly wrong and out of sight

God is the greatest sinner of us all
God is the greatest monster of us all
God is the greatest violator of us all
God is the greatest bully of us all

Chapter Three

and by the way cutting off the foreskin
and throwing it in a bin
was not a procedure invented by yhwh
it had for a long time been the way

we have been schooled
and we have been fooled
into believing that God is all knowing
even as the devil is in his kayak rowing

one male God that looks like us
someone who apparently does not even cuss
and everything everywhere is known by him
even when we dance naked in the club on a whim

I don't think so my friend
to that belief I will not bend
what a stupid thing to think
not even worth a blink

God supposedly sees all things great and small
even when your girlfriend makes a call
to another lover and expresses her lust
and later exposes her bust

how can that be
everything he cannot see
he can't even keep track of me
as I'm trying to be free

come on people use your brain
which acts mostly as a sewage drain
because you act so dense
and reject common sense

tradition has you in its grasp
it makes you wheez and gasp
pulling you into the cesspool of unbelievable crap
and compelling your brain to take a nap

sleep on oh stupid pilgrim
your ignorance is vile and grim
you uphold a god who's filled with hate
whose treachery will not abate

promising to send most people to hell is what he
teaches
calling himself a god of love is what he preaches
but the proof is in his history
and about that there is no mystery

but look behold angels in the heavens singing
and flying shepherds singing
from the east there are wise men fornicating
and also they are hallucinating

behold a virgin shall conceive
the devil she will deceive
with apocalyptic echoes she shall proceed
to bring forth a royal seed

and they shall call his name great
and they shall call on his name with hate
and they shall nail him to a repurposed crate
and all evil will abate

yes it was a scheme
and furthermore it was a dream
the ancients were filled with illusions
as they forged all manner of collusions

who is this God that boasts of almighty power
where is his wonderful tower
we've read about his incredible story
but never have we seen his glory

the invention of gods was a necessary part
where else would we start
to try to explain the mysteries
and our histories

look at the twilights last gleaming
and the movies that are streaming
and tell me if God is there
or anywhere

here a god there a god
all of them a fraud
invented by strange and possessed souls
and weirdo dysfunctional trolls

dam mr.sheetakovsky it's a bloody mess
with antie dodo asking for a caress
all she got was a massage from the priest
and a spiritual feast

there were once upon a time a lot more
gods like Thor
where did they go
I'd like to know

and where was yhwh all that time
not yet in his prime
or not born yet
what are the odds and who wants to bet

the truth is that gods have always been fabricated
by fertile minds and then desecrated
by others who invented their own versions
who then fought each other for conversions

religions were created to glorify the gods they made
with sacrifices and rituals which paid
for all the sins that they committed
so they all could be forgiven and aquitted

the appearance finally of this God yhwh was part of a
long evolution
part of a revolution
as mankind wallowing in indecision
expanded their vision

the people wanted a God who had might
who stood up and said let there be light
as he gave form to a world that was formless
and showed himself to be supreme and enormous

some worshipped the sun
they thought it'd be a lot of fun
while others bowed down to the moon
that's what made them swoon

on and on it went in history
imaginations making up the story
and building upon foundations of myth
with expensive theories that went with

and finally out of histories mist
appeared a God who was really pissed
tough and jealous and mean
he remained completely unseen

leaving us to imagine what he really looked like
and shielding ourselves in case he should strike
he caused us to tremble and fear
and bring out a bottle of beer

Chapter four

they all made fun of Noah when he built an ark
everyone thought it was a great big lark
but then the rains came and they all cried
and everyone died

nice move God to kill most of your peeps
you'd think to do that only to creeps
but there were also children drowning in the rain
you must have been quite insane

and this is what a god of love does
pardon me if I'm quite outraged because
I'd be a big fool
if I thought that this was cool

this is quite the god that the Israelites conjured up
a real lover of people buttercup
step right up to get your hug of the day
then stone some people down by the bay

gotta be nimble and gotta be quick
to stay away from a god so sick
if you disobey a word he says
with his sword he quickly slays

if this is love then rescue me
from this tyrant I want to be free
hide me in the rocks and hills
and give me some nice pink pills

I fear this God who kills and maims
and calls us nasty barbaric names
he rules with anger and he makes us fear
we're always scared and shedding a tear

pass me not oh gentle saviour
son of God do me a favor
please die for me upon a cross
and be the new and loving boss

a potion was foretold of a saving grace
but only for the Jews that master race
an envoy would go down and die
their freedom he would buy

god did not invent the rules that in his law were laid
that other nations had long ago made
it was all a natural evolution of human thought
there was nothing new that the Israelites brought

Israel was a tiny collection of tribes
run by gangsters and bribes
they became a kingdom under Saul their king
but it soon fell apart doodly schnoodly ping

just because God is barbaric and mean
is not proof that he doesn't exist or is lean
but because he is barbaric and mean
it's wrong to call him a god of love even if he's clean

he's promised to torture those who don't obey him
forever
that's not cool ever
so clearly he has not evolved into a good dude
and that's just rude

he talks about being good and not sinning
and for the bums no binning
but he himself does ethnic cleansing, torturing and
murder for hire
and for fun he'll slash your tire

it's true so cry
it's true and not a lie
it's true oh me oh my
it's true bye bye

friendly fire coming down the line
and for that they'll get a massive fine
so smarten up and run and hide
it smells like someone died

chalk it up to youthful exuberance and guilt
and be thankful for your mothers quilt
she made it just for you oh wretched soul
now go and listen to your rock and roll

and pray to God for bread to eat
as you listen to your Devils beat
he might smite you as you dance
or cause you to fall down as you prance

Jerusalem Jerusalem how many are the tears I cried
for thee
if only you listened to my voice where would you be
but you walked in paths of unrighteousness alone
as I watched you it caused me to moan

the bible defines who God is
and he's not a transvestite named Liz
he's mr.supremo who lives in heaven
who loves the number seven

did you hear the one about the donkey that talked
how about the shark that walked
and then there was Jonah for three days in the whale
worse than living in a jail

God is all about the glory
he loves a great story
for a bigger punch throw in a few miracles
or a few oracles

I ran to the river to pray
I felt so good that I stayed all day
and then Alice came and brought me some wine
together we had a jolly good time

and as we drank we talked about life
how we were tired of all the strife
we longed for peace and happiness and joy
that would nice oh boy oh boy

Chapter Five

heaven is a wonderful place
filled with glory and grace
I want to see God's holy face
way up there in outer space

one plus ten equals eleven
and I wonder where is heaven
it used to be above the blue canopy
but now from our ignorance we're free

does Yahweh ever drink
or play with his dink
what about drugs to feel good
or going dancing in his hood

maybe he was drunk when he did the flood
he did say he was sorry - pass another bud
never again he said
see my rainbow and now it's off to bed

God doesn't really have a bed cause he never sleeps
he hangs out with his angel peeps
and watches his people on earth
which never cause him mirth

humans make God mad
they make him sad
even his Jews are causing him pain
he wants to wack them with a cane

in the old days he had neighboring armies attack the
chosen ones
because they were practicing idolatry and pinching
foreign buns
dam those Israelites he cursed
as his temper burst

if my people who are called by my name
would stop playing that silly game
where they disobey my rules
then I would forgive the stupid fools

once upon a time there was Daniel in the lions den
and the lions didn't eat him in their pen
what a miracle says the preacher
amazing shouts the teacher

and what about the three guys in the fiery furnace
the flames didn't even kill them so that's a case
where God intervened and saved them
now that story is a real gem

when Satan was a little boy
God bought him a nice little toy
little lucifer loved his brand new gun
and loved to shoot at the sun

on heavens golden streets walk the saints in gold attire
all of them having gone through the fire
now they drink iced tea and reminisce
and use the golden toilet to take a piss

and the earth was without form and void
no humans - not even a Lloyd
so god went to work
and the female demons began to twerk

but he did not get distracted
nor did he get attracted
not even when he was photographed by a guy named
bob
who was trying to influence the job

on the seventh God took a break
it was good so he went and had some cake
God said yummy
yummy for my tummy

and then the problems began with the serpent
tempting eve
promising her sex with a guy named Steve
she declined and instead had a piece of fruit
and for that God gave her the boot

you and Adam get out of here
and forget about having a beer
you've sinned and now you have to pay the price
I see now that you're not so nice

go and smoke your weed
you will suffer for your bad deed
no nice garden for you guys
and no heaven in the skies

one day it was snowing in heaven and God was
drinking Fanta
and in walked this guy called Santa
and God said what's up Stan
and Santa said that's not my name man

okay replied God welcome here
and do you want a beer
and Santa said yes I do
and God said look at you

Santa put a gift under the tree
and sang da da da dee
merry Christmas to all in sight
and to all a good night

and so the first Christmas was born
as an angel played on his horn
and God said lets do this every year
it will bring us all good cheer

and it was December twenty five
and the angles were doing the jive
and God was thinking of redeeming mankind
cause everything on earth was in a bind

God wanted to save the humans from hell
especially the farmer in the dell
there's got to be a way
I wonder what the wise men have to say

he summoned them from the east
and put on a lavish feast
they told him to sacrifice his son
and he said - consider it done

over this decision he cried many tears
as he was beset with fears
what if the humans don't get it
and everything goes for shit

it's going to be a gamble
to fail would be a shamble
but I've got to give it a try
otherwise my creations going to fry

but there's time for that yet
I'm willing to bet
for now we'll celebrate Christmas time
and make all our words rhyme

oh Christmas tree
what do you see
when in our living rooms you do appear
I hope you sense good cheer

I think God invented Christmas as he was scheming
of his son Jesus he was dreaming
thinking about how mankind he could save
and that his son would have to be very brave

to go down to earth and get strung up on a cross
what a terrible loss
there would be a lot of pain
it really would be insane

and so it was that a long time before the Christ
appeared
God made up his mind to do the thing he feared
to save mankind from eternal death
and give them eternal breath

Chapter Six

the humans at one point wanted more power
so they built a tall tower
to reach God was their desire
but they were playing with fire

God caused them all in different tongues to speak
some of them even began to squeak
and he chased them to other parts
throwing at them fiery darts

he told them to take a hike
especially a tall guy with big ears named mike
shoo shoo he yelled as they fled
serves you right he said as they bled

some spoke Hebrew and some spoke French
others said nothing and sat on a bench
still others spoke Spanish and Greek
while others paddled up the old Russian creek

it was the greatest fiasco since the death of Abel
and they called it the Tower of Babel
but of course it was a big fat lie
it's enough to make one cry

it appears that God got scared when the people
united
in him great fear was ignited
he thought they would eventually reach him in the
sky dome
up in heaven where he made his home

we know now why the sky is blue
how space stretched forever no matter how high you
flew
the bible writers didn't have a clue
what can you do

no matter how you choose to look
it's just another myth in the bible book
put together by ancients over time
with little real meaning or rhyme

but the god they made up was such a clueless twit
about life he didn't know shit
and that's to be expected from a god that's invented
who's more than a little demented

shadows play on the neon sign in the ghettos
as Peggy Sue staggers home on her stilettos
but she did enjoy all the food and wine
all in all it was pretty fine

life is a strange journey in the dark
with everyone acting like it's all a lark
somehow we've lost the connection to our brain
with everyone acting insane

people want to go their own way
even when it's a cloudy rainy day
it's with much gusto that they enter many fights
all to protect their basic human rights

bend oh puny human to my will
come now please take this little pill
and when you do all will be fine
and we'll have croissants and cheese and some nice
red wine

read my law and obey it to the letter
otherwise I'll whip you with a nasty netter
and you'll be bleeding from your head to your toe
looking like a total schmo

why not just give in
and stop your will to sin
step out from your filthy bin
and have some tonic and gin

we'll drink a toast to the sweet bye and bye
where you'll never have to cry
all you have to do is just comply
and never tell another selfish lie

if you obey you go to heaven
if you don't you go to hell where you'll have to count
to seven
it's either comply
or you will fry

God said its his way or the highway
there is no other byway
there's no place where one can go and hide
even for those who've died

Chapter Seven

one two three four five six seven
I saw a ghost on my way to heaven
she smiled at me and showed me her tits
it tore my heart to bits

do you think that ghosts are real
or just some kind of crazy spiel
seen by lunatics and off beat guys
and disrespected Russian spies

in the haunted house they prowl
in the attic we hear them growl
they glide so effortlessly along the hall
and make us feel so small

I think that God was sad
he was an artist gone mad
across the universe his paints he flung
in Jupiter his hymns were sung

his creativity knew no bounds
he made cats and rats and bloodhounds
loving light he made the stars
loving darkness he made the bars

drink well oh cheerless pilgrim in this barren land
grab your instrument and play in the Jesus band
let your musical genius percolate and shine
wash it all down with some Italian red wine

God took on human form to come to earth
he did so for Adam and Eve's birth
with them in the garden he walked
and talked

in heaven God has a different form
maybe he looks like a trooper of storm
we don't know how he looks
or even what he cooks

but I think he visits us from time to time
maybe as a jester or a mime
or perhaps as a Mendelssohn or a Brahms
showing us that for good music he has no qualms

angles are with him when he comes
to protect him from all the bums
that roam around and act like dummies
who didn't listen to their mummies

see Sarah walk down the street with her poodle
she's just eaten a big piece of streudle
she wants to go home and canoodle
and then sit down and doodle

at the city of ninevah they relented
all their evil deeds they recanted
so God didn't send down the fire
and Jonah became a crier

why god why did you not them all destroy
I was dreaming of it boy oh boy
I spent three days inside a fish
to see them destroyed was my wish

so Jonah sat by the way and sulked like a child
he was clearly very riled
he was called to give a warning to the sinners
but he didn't want them to be winners

so we see that God forgave the sinners who were
doing meth
and spared them from destruction and death
but why would he want to kill them at all
why would he make that call

God a philosopher is not
he's a writer inventing a plot
creating characters and a story
all for his own glory

he's not the only God around
it's says so in the scriptures turn up the sound
but he wants to be number one
otherwise he's not having fun

why do you think him and lucifer fought
it's because old luc got caught
talking a lot of smack
behind yhwh's back

that really made him cross
and so he acted like a boss
and kicked his number one out the door
threatening him with a whole lot more

Satan took a lot of angels with him when he left
with his tongue he was very deft
and that really pissed the father off
it even made him cough

and so they fight for the humans soul
as Satan invented rock and roll
and God chooses to listen to gospel hymns
while his angels work out in heavens gyms

onward Christian soldiers march to Zion
and pretend you are a lion
to defeat the devil and his demons is the cause
keep on hating and don't push pause

it's an endless war with yhwh
fighting Satan is the way
where is all the peace they talk about
where is all the joy I hear them shout

with this religion it's killing and judgement and
destruction
no one talking about new construction
take it down and tear down the tent
it's time to cry and vent

Moses ran around the camp and slaughtered
thousands with his sword
he was mad about the golden calf and so was his lord
no other gods before me
now do you see

ya we see cause it's a bloody mess
very troubling I must confess
God is a bloodthirsty guy for sure
so don't go and be a whore

no selling your body for money girl
not even to a priest or an earl
it's a sinful thing to do
don't you have a clue

and no fornicating behind the shed
ya we're talking about you Ned
stay away from sister rose
and don't go playing with your hose

if we find out that someone has been boned
then the participants will be stoned
isn't that a little harsh
why not just drown them in a marsh

man oh man this God is tough
man oh man this God is rough
man oh man this God don't take no guff
man oh man this God will give you a cuff

Chapter Eight

I see the vampires on the evening news
they've all been paying their spiritual dues
they're waiting for Armageddon so they can drink
blood
as it flows from the humans like a flood

they think that day is fast approaching
as God mankind keeps on reproaching
and it's just as it was in the days of Noah
with the wagon trains hitching up in Shenandoah

soon it will be time to run for the hills
as God comes to collect all the bills
the trumpets will sound and the dead will arise
better change your ways if you are wise

why does God want to destroy part of the world and
a lot of mankind
why is he intent on judgement and revenge instead of
acting kind
it's totally insane and uncivilized
with billions victimized

that such a god is a creator does not make sense
he would have to be super dense
a crackpot and a monster barbarian
and a nasty two faced sectarian

why did God not give Adam a computer at his birth
it would have increased his net worth
invest in Apple it would say
there is no other way

after some time along came Cain and Abel
before there was the tower of Babel
Cain got jealous and poor Abel he killed
he should have just chilled

God was still talking to the first family at this time
and he asked Cain what he had done this time
I just killed my brother this time
you've gone too far this time

Cain's dog began to bark
when God put on Cain a mark
wander around you stupid knave
go and live in a cold damp cave

Cain was a forerunner of all the monks
who isolate themselves and sleep in stone bunks
they are weird as hell and love to beat
drums and especially their meat

monks like to be alone and study and pray
I think that's okay
they're mysterious and secluded and soon
we'll see them all walking on the moon

the bible thought the moon was its own light
the scribes were not too bright
God told them what to write
he didn't even know that he was not right

let's face it this God they made up only knew what
they knew
and that wasn't much so they guessed as all ancients do
what did they know about gravity and stars
or Venus or Jupiter or Mars

superstition lives within the human soul
encouraged by the music of rock and roll
the old woman asks if she can read your palms
and you say you have no qualms

what does your horoscope say
will you have a great day
and what's your sign
is it the same as mine

don't walk underneath a ladder please
cover your mouth when you sneeze
watch out for the black cat
how about that

belief in Yahweh is a case of suspended disbelief
it's enjoyable to believe in the fantasy - good grief
throw your hands up in the air
and stop and stare

there goes Yahweh riding in his chariot up high
throwing down some thunderbolts oh my
I think I got him mixed up with Thor
in the end it's all such a bore

but some love the adventure and the fantasy
it makes them feel protected and la dee dee
giddy with sanctimonious pretension
they give their minds a suspension

oh mortal give your head a shake
why do you believe in what the ancients tried to bake
a good cake is such a tasty treat
and a real god would be fun to meet

we need to sponsor you an intervention
to extract you from this God who's such a recent
invention
why do you feel
that he is real

and then along came peter
a big pumpkin eater
who invented the pope
another crazy dope

put on your dress dear Martha Von papst
sit in the closet and drink your peach schnapps
soon you'll be tipsy and out of your tree
it really will be something to see

the atheists waltz in with their vampires in tow
it seems that they got into a row
with Christians and politicians and belligerent Jews
all of them proclaiming different views

dear count what is it that you have read
about your relatives who are long since dead
who cares that they loved to dance
just relax and stop and give it a chance

history befuddles and confuses us all
our history books all seem to be small
so many details are missing from its pages
and so many wise old sages

believe me they cry with outstretched hands
why don't you give in to their demands
they scream from the rooftops with hearts on fire
demanding not to be considered a liar

everybody has a hood
where it's about evil and good
there's a good guy
and there's a bad guy

the bible says God is the good guy
and the devil is the bad guy
there's a competition going on here
what'll it be - whiskey or beer

tow the line with God or go with Satan and sin
go with Satan and you're not in
you're out
go ahead and pout

punishment and reward
or go into the mental ward
your choice as well
but when you're born you're already condemned to
hell

babies in hell my friend
that's what it is in the end
and God says he's a nice guy
that's something I don't buy

say one thing and do something else is what God does
because
God condemns babies to hell
and then says that he's a God of love as well

double talk and misplaced trust
glass of water and a day old crust
take your shiny nickel plated platter
throw it on the ground and listen to it clatter

Chapter Nine

if God is changeless how does he adapt to a changing
moral landscape
he wears a hoodie and puts on a cape
look at me I can fly
way up high

gods morality matched those of his inventors which
were so unkind
but as times changed he got left behind
and so it was that the messiah syndrome came into
play
which gave the people a say

we need a saviour to save us from Rome
it's getting unbearable here underneath the dome
who will bring us life and hope
who will help us all to cope

behold a Virgin shall conceive and bear a son and
hostilities shall cease
and his name shall be called Prince of peace
he will defeat the Romans and restore Israel to her
rightful place
so she can send astronauts to outer space

Bethlehem was the chosen site
where God flew his heavenly kite
at the Manger was born a newborn king
the son of God was he and the Angels did sing

wise men came and shepherds too
even a clown snuck in and said boo
and so the plan was set in motion
even as Mary put on some baby lotion

what a splendid plan the Angels remarked
even as Pilates dog stood at the door and barked
you found a way to save your creation
and bring redemption to the nation

the snow was falling and the child nuzzled
but in New York City the people were puzzled
why is the son of God born at the lowly Manger
treated like an outcast and a stranger

Mary and Joseph should have been booked at the
Bethlehem Hotel
not at the cheap Manger Motel
this King of kings and lord of lords
should have been feted on the billboards

attention oh Israel your redeemer has been born
on this chilly December morn
it's the second Christmas ever
and we will not forget never

but there were precious few
who knew
that God had come down to earth
as Mary had given birth

no screaming headlines in the local papers
no politicians making hay and doing capers
no trumpets blasting out the news
no high priests paying their dues

only a few
knew
shepherds and angels and wise men
all in all very zen

no one toasting Jesus at the bar
but how about that star
standing right there above the place
a miraculous case

over at the mall Santa was greeted with a cheer
no one knew why he was here
but he brought gifts and some candy cane
and shook his big white mane

meanwhile at the Chelsea hotel the philosophers sang
as the chambermaids ears rang
there was a feeling in the air
that God had begun to care

as they sipped their coffee and smoked their pot
they realized that it was not
business as usual in the world
and everyone's hair got curled

holy was the day
blessed was the way
humility was shown
and the pot was homegrown

God believed in child sacrifice
it was not nice
and so he sent his only son to be killed
so the law could be fulfilled

that's how the new story went
down to earth the son was sent
preaching a message of forgiveness and love
in the air you see the dove

what a silly story
and all that glory
borrowing from other cultures bit by bit
to make it sound legit

the plan was to have judas betray the Christ
that's bizarre and it's a heist
poor guy didn't stand a chance
it was all a pre planned dance

and how is a crucifixion a sacrifice
it doesn't suffice
It wasn't nice
but it wasn't a sacrifice

one man can't die for everyone and their cat
what kind of a stupid concept is that
it's made up crap
a spiritual trap

got you silly and foolish and stupid believers
you've been had by the deceivers
those fraudulent daydream perceivers
high on spiritual fevers

let's see how can we make this religion more in tune
where our ideas don't belong out on the moon
we can't have a god so harsh
a god that shoots alligators in the marsh

we need forgiveness and a way back
for a condemned humanity that lives in a sack
aha the virgin model will work
everyone party and twerk

was it a conspiracy or just an evolution of religion
let's change things just a smidgen
the people will believe anything
so they gave God an offspring

the son of God to the rescue of the Yahweh concept
his supposed sacrifice to accept
and thereby circumnavigate the law with its rules
inventing new and more refined schools

Peter denied it as he rolled the dice
the rooster crowed thrice
he walked away in shame
he had sullied his masters name

such a crock
even called a rock
such a dope
and now we have the pope

wear your dress oh master of disguise what do you
care
as you swing your incense container in the air
and please put on your goofy hat
you're as black and sinister as a bat

oh look how the trolls dance underneath the bridge
bring me the money and let's climb up upon that
ridge
from whence we can catch a glimpse of Calvary
and dream of being free

Chapter Ten

it's all so very primeval
this imaginary battle between good and evil
God is good la dee da
Satan is bad la dee da

evil is a moniker that is meaningless
evil is the perception of sinister forces that are
spiritual distress
evil has to do with always doing bad things
evil is a description of bad behaviour

God is not good or he wouldn't have killed innocent
children right
if you can't see that well then you're not very bright
if anyone is evil then God is
they drank the pop but there was no fiz

no fiz my friend
no path to the end
no way to mend
no way to lend

where is satan's book where he explains his actions in
all of this
about his relations with Yahweh in this
ongoing story about the great fight
between wrong and right

lucifer that great angel can't be all bad
his angels can't be so sad
and who knows who's going to win
amongst all this din

the bible talks about many gods having a meeting
and lucifer was also there getting a greeting
so obviously God is not the only one up there
there are others too with God in the air

but the bible wants us to believe that Yahweh is the
greatest one of all
of course he's got the biggest ball
everyone wants their God to be the big daddy
and not be hanging around as somebody's caddy

Baal and El were there before Yahweh
where did he come from on that sunny day in May
he evolved along with mankinds imaginative story
creating a new deity for a new people and their glory

maestro please the E-Chord
please prepare ye the way of the lord
lo he cometh on clouds of glory
to fulfill the foretelling of history

she sat next to me smoking her crack
I read her my poetry and scratched her back
it was like a dream
and we were on a spiritual team

Jesus Christ are you the superstar from the father
should I follow you or not bother
are you the manifestation of a new way
creating for all of us a better day

sunshine and roses all day long
the lord making us happy and strong
forgiven of all of the things we did wrong
even as we take a drag from our bong

peaceful feelings and sacred yellow smoke
baby please pass me that toke
I'm sure the lord would approve
and get himself into the groove

groovy Jesus we love you
with you we don't have to feel blue
we dance in praise to you
and prance about cause we love you too

sell all you have and follow me
the rich young ruler couldn't see
his way clear to let it all go
so he hung his head and kept all of his dough

you demand too much oh Jesus of Gallilee
you want it all that I can see
you ask that we give up our lives
and listen to the beggars cries

accept me as your sacrifice
I'll turn you into someone nice
and the father will accept you into the fold
as long as you do what you are told

you would have to be intellectually disabled to
believe in a virgin birth
but of such stories there is no dirth
it's a template from ancient times
to find a scapegoat to pay for the people's crimes

those who came after Jesus used it as well
inventing and cobbling together a story in the dell
hey farmer come look and see what I found
I'm sure when you see it will astound

St. Paul saw the light
what a fright
a godly sight
a potion of heavens might

Paul why do you persecute me
I am the messiah why can't you see
go and find this Christian and he will pray
so you can see again and serve me in my way

another miracle to make this story work
another conversion by a guy who was a jerk
he persecuted the Christians and got them stoned
and now his gross sin has been atoned

why does blood have to be shed for the remission of
sins
it's prehistoric nonsense that should be thrown in
the stupid bins
we've grown up and don't need this crap
oh oh here comes God - zap zap

the evolution of mankind came complete with the
God syndrome
and we felt at home
with this tradition and invented our own versions
complete with conversions

we came from very barbaric roots
look at Sam and how he shoots
animals for pleasure
and then hangs up their heads like a treasure

Jesus and his generation were changing
the law they were rearranging
looking for a changer
looking for a manger

every God is a reflection of the society that creates
him or her
and sooner or later they dispense with him or her
we see that in history
that's the real story

Yahweh is no different and in time he will be gone
replaced with someone or some other con
life moves on
find another pawn

in the bookcase the spirt of the age was stirring
ideas were in the air whirring
watch the philosophers bend down and pick
something up in the mud
maybe a piece of crud

a revolution is always brewing
as in the woods the witches are stewing
four horses livers and swatch of raccoon hair
throw it in the pot and see if we care

on the holy mountain God is writing a new plan
which he will give to a man named Stan
who will nail it to the temple door
where it will become part of the new age lore

Chapter Eleven

give me your hand
and let me lead you to the promised land
where the streets are made of gold
and you will never get old

it's a promise that reeks of spice
and everything that's nice
it's hard to dismiss it as folklore
and even harder to ignore

it all goes south if you reject this offer
and turn into a scoffer
down you go to the Devil's lair
where the fires of hell will singe your hair

no streets of gold but red hot ore
as you scream and howl forevermore
help me Jesus you will cry
please just let me die

but the pain will never stop
no break for even a bee bop
we can't imagine this unending torture
and for its pain there is no cure

the carrot and the stick going round and round
God flogging his creation pound for pound
take this nasty human
didn't you know there was a ban

obey my commandments or else you'll pay the price
and I promise I won't be nice
all will not go well
as I torture you in hell

neon lights in heaven shining bright
and all the prophets getting tight
reading scripture and getting the meanings right
while they stand underneath a golden light

Heaven is an experience that goes on day by day
with nobody looking for a new way
does heaven revolve or rotate
and is God ever late

sorry I'm late for the meeting
but here I am to give you my greeting
let's hear it for the saints
hope they win the Super Bowl next year

come on boy won't you rattle my chain
prove to me that you're not insane
recite the latest blast from the past
and then continue your fast

it's absurd to think that everything happened by
chance
someone had to define this dance
and so we invent gods to explain how
then sit down and eat some chow

millions of gods have been invented over time
none of them are real but it's not a crime
no one knows what's really going on
so we embrace every new con

to say there is no higher power is a lie
even though our questioning makes us sigh
the atheists are also in the dark
as up a strange tree they bark

Yahweh is the latest God in a long line
some bad and some fine
but sooner or later they went away
and another entered the fray

in the middle of the night frank counted his money
then he woke his wife and said hey honey
let's go on a vacation to the North Pole
imagine that could be our goal

his wife let put a sigh and kicked him out of the bed
he fell on the ground and thought he was dead
but he wasn't and he went to the couch
and took some tobacco from a pouch

he filled his pipe and started to smoke
and then he began to choke
his wife yelled at him to stop all the noise
and to stop playing with his toys

he put his pipe away and lay down and slept
as he rested he wept
and then he dreamed of riches
and making out with some bitches

then he woke up and his wife told him to get to work
get to work you silly jerk
and don't wake me up in the night
I don't want to see the light

gonna get high
with the spirit in the sky
with a box full of candies
which will be handed out by a bunch of dandies

God don't like people who are strange
especially those from the shacks on the range
they walk funny like willy
and talk very silly

is he not a puppet master supreme
someone who's always skimming off the cream
creating tough guys like Samson
who kisses Delilah and takes a run

all the cool kids played in the band
the smart ones played in the sand
the geniuses made a demand
that the professors should be canned

then some ghost riders were sent to the Sinai
they were sent there by Adonai
he is great
and he will determine your fate

once upon a time there was a ghoul
he liked to relax down by the pool
drinking at the bar and sitting on his stool
and acting cool

deep in the forest lived a hermit
he didn't like people even a little bit
so he meditated on the Lord
and listened to the lion as it roared

with the breastplate of righteousness on we carry on
the fight
to serve God and shine the light
so all people will accept Jesus and do what's right
and make the world super duper bright

the archangel blows his horn
as heavens creatures look forlorn
they all look to the throne
where God is laughing and talking on the phone

God is as real as the pants that you wear
and he cries when you walk around bare
so put your pants on and be cool
cause if you don't believe in God you're a great big
fool

Chapter Twelve

still from the pulpit the pastor keeps on preaching
about the truth of the Word he keeps on teaching
he is a true believer
in god and the deceiver

one cannot shake his deep convictions
even when faced with all the contradictions
he stands resolute and strong
refusing to admit that the bible is wrong

wrong about this and wrong about that
it's as if he's blind as a bat
encased in a bubble of make belief and mythology
clinging fervently to his doxology

religion dulls the human soul
to imprison all people is it's goal
it puts on perfume and fancy clothes
and ties it's hair in ribbons and bows

and millions buy into its nefarious plots
they plant their feet within its pots
crying please water me and help me grow
so someday I will to heaven go

but what about the nonsense of Noah and the ark
that story is such a lark
simply based on older myths like Gilgamesh
so then let's all go to Bangladesh

let's all go and have ourselves a beer
but let's not shoot ourselves a deer
we can eat some pizza and some soup
and then we'll have to find a place to poop

I can't believe the endless lies
even as I eat my pumpkin pies
lies and pies they taste so good
when you dine with friends in the neighbourhood

but why are people so dense
to believe all this nonsense
what happened to their brain
did it turn into a massive drain

oh me oh my what can we do
to help those who don't have a clue
brainwashed they are by pastors nuns and priests
I wish they'd think a bit at least

evolution took billions of years
getting drunk takes a few dozen beers
the bible doesn't have a clue
what is a person to do

how can one believe in manna from the sky
next week it'll be a big old apple pie
these stories are not true
I'm going to the loo

to the loo
to the loo
to hide my head
and wish I was dead

not really but the frustration grows
as my amazement grows
that people still believe all this stuff
I've just about had enough

oh the silliness that it takes
to believe that a god named yhwh bakes
banana fudge cakes
a lot of brainlessness that takes

Chapter Thirteen

one god listens to everyone's prayers at the same time
to believe that should be a crime
does that make sense to you
and will you dance right on cue

when the apologists play hymns upon their harps
trying to convince the doubters that underneath
heavens tarps
nuggets of truths are being grown
to prove that god can hear everyone all alone

common sense we need
for clarity we plead
confusion reigns in Christian camps
as lying minds snuff out the lamps

the darkness of deception is what religion brings
with endless lies our soul it stings
it bullies us and beats us down
it's a self righteous religious fascist takedown

the priests and pastors got the power
they condemn the doubters to the tower
they threaten us with the fires of hell
as they pretend to ring heavens bell

repent repent they cry
as all the sinners sigh
they scare the weak into the fold
while rattling the cages of the strong and bold

we are gods servants here on earth
better listen to us if you want a rebirth
they intimidate as they do their dance
expecting the people to get up and prance

Chapter Fourteen

in clouds of joy we smile and walk
keeping our eyes upon the clock
tic toc it says as we do our work
and try to humour uncle dirk

at times we labour on into the night
at times we nearly die of fright
at times we try with all our might
at times we're filled with great delight

when we were young we all believed
that god from us our prayers received
and that he loved us and he cared
as to him our souls we bared

we grew up and what a shame
we learned that he didn't know our name
we couldn't call him on the phone
we had to make it on our own

there was no need to set us free
there was no sacrifice at Calvary
no god up there to cause us pain
no one up there driving us insane

we all are free and no one died
we all are free and no one cried
no one was lost so no one was found
no one by sin was enslaved and bound

an abstract god was created so we could explain
things like death and storms and pain
but now we've advanced and know what's true
no need to stand in all that poo

holy smokes the bum is in the bin
rummaging around to try to find a sin
he sniffs and with his hand does grope
so he can find one and buy some hope

the shoes are in the mud and the maker's in the grave
look over yonder at the monk in his cave
give the nun a shilling for a half-pint of gin
and pay father brown a nickel for your sin

www.ingramcontent.com/pod-product-compliance
Lightning Source LLC
Chambersburg PA
CBHW031521040426
42445CB00009B/330